A VERY KROLL CHRISTMAS

BETTY PARASKEVAS

ILLUSTRATED BY MICHAEL PARASKEVAS

HARCOURT BRACE & COMPANY

SAN DIEGO NEW YORK LONDON

Copyright © 1994 by Rita E. Paraskevas and
Michael P. Paraskevas

Requests for permission to make copies of any
part of the work should be mailed to: Permissions
Department, Harcourt Brace & Company, 6277
Sea Harbor Drive, Orlando, Florida 32887-6777.

Library of Congress
Cataloging-in-Publication Data
Paraskevas, Betty.
A very Kroll Christmas/Betty Paraskevas;
illustrated by Michael Paraskevas.—1st ed. p. cm.
Summary: A collection of poems describes
how Junior Kroll and his family get ready for
Christmas.
ISBN 0-15-292883-9
1. Christmas—Juvenile poetry. 2. Children's
poetry, American. [1. Christmas—Poetry.
2. American poetry. 3. Humorous poetry.]
I. Paraskevas, Michael, 1961–   ill. II. Title.
PS3566.A627V47 1994 811'.54—dc20   93-41624
First edition   A B C D E

The illustrations in this book were done in
gouache on bristol board.
The display type was hand-lettered by the
illustrator.
The text type was set in Simoncini Garamond by
Harcourt Brace & Company Photocomposition
Center, San Diego, California.
Color separations were made by Bright Arts,
Ltd., Singapore.
Printed and bound by Tien Wah Press, Singapore
Production supervision by Warren Wallerstein
and Kent MacElwee
Designed by Michael Farmer

Printed in Singapore

To Connie Boucher:
Thank you for being Determined.

And to Donald Wilkes:
Sometimes opportunity doesn't knock,
it wanders in through the door.

—B. P. and M. P.

KICKING OFF THE CHRISTMAS SEASON

Junior Kroll surrendered a sigh—
Mom did it again, the turkey was dry.
Aunt Jane brought that lumpy cranberry sauce.
Let's have the canned stuff and give that a toss.
Where did they dig up these relatives?
　　Not a single one could hear.
They arrived every Thanksgiving Day,
　　then disappeared till the following year.
Cousin Honey Duff stuck out her tongue
　　and made that nasty sound
While Colonel Pickle was saying grace.
　　Now she's nowhere to be found.
Grandfather's cousin Mabel
　　served her famous chowder.

She's kinda nice but awfully fat,
  and she smells like talcum powder.
Pass the peas, pass the rolls.
Hallelujah! Bless the Krolls.
Wait a minute! What's the joke?
Mom looks like she's about to choke.
Aunt Jane's laughing in her napkin.
  Dad's face is turning red.
Oh, no, Mr. Wiener's curly toupee
  is slipping off his head.
Mashed potatoes, sweet potatoes,
  cauliflower, beets.
What does cousin Mabel mean,
  "A brussels sprout repeats"?

Praise the Lord, dinner's over.
    Junior Kroll is humming.
There's one good thing about Thanksgiving—
    It means that Christmas is coming.

THE CHRISTMAS BAZAAR

Junior Kroll hopped out of the car,
Told Mom he'd walk home from the Christmas bazaar.
It was just for kids. There were gifts to buy,
Hot apple cider and hot apple pie.
For a dollar you got a present and a chance to chat
With Santa Claus, whose head was too small for his hat.
He wasn't fat and jolly, but tall and very thin,
And Junior saw a space between his whiskers and his chin.
Junior watched the other kids open the presents they got.
He decided to keep his money. The gifts didn't look so hot.
He was waiting in line for the hot apple pie
    when someone began to holler.
That bully, Ray Tupper, didn't like his gift
    and demanded back his dollar.
Santa dragged Ray Tupper straight across the floor.
Ray shouted, "KROLL, I'LL BE WAITING FOR YOU,
    RIGHT OUTSIDE THE DOOR!"

Junior was trapped. What could he do?
He looked around for someone he knew.
There was Mrs. Green with some hot apple cider.
He walked right over and sat down beside her.
Wouldn't she like him to walk her home?
It just wasn't safe out there alone.
Together they stepped into the night.
Mrs. Green gushed, he was awfully polite,
Especially for someone so extremely young.
But she didn't see Junior stick out his tongue
At the shadowy figure behind the Wise Men.
Junior'd outfoxed that bully again.

WE NEED A LITTLE CHRISTMAS

Junior Kroll found some bells
  and tied them to his laces.
After a while his Christmas spirit
  began to show upon the faces
Of Mom and Dad. *Ting-a-ling,*
  up and down the stairs.
Along the halls, through the walls,
  underneath the chairs.
If, by chance, the bells stopped ringing,
The anticipation of the *ting-a-ling*ing
Was just as bad.
But Mom and Dad
Were reluctant to tamper with so precious a thing
As Junior's spirit. They let the bells ring.
With seven busy days to go,
Crazy Max began to show
Signs of stress. Each time he'd snooze,
Those bells would ring and he'd blow a fuse.
When Junior rose one day at dawn
And reached for his shoes, the bells were gone!
He examined the laces. "Elementary," he said.
"I know who took my bells, and he's under my bed."
And just beyond Junior's grasp, Max was fast asleep,
Lost in the land of a thousand trees, dreaming of marshmallow sheep.
Poor Junior Kroll, his bells won't ring.
Not till the tulips bloom in the spring.

BAKER EXTRAORDINAIRE

Junior Kroll stirs the bowl:
    butter, sugar, eggs, and flour.
He's baking cookies while Mrs. Kroll
    is napping for an hour.
Straight from the bottle
    he pours in vanilla,
As he sings "Silent Night,
    Holy Night" a capella.
Hurry! Get the baking trays
    and the rolling pin.
Shake a little flour out.
    Roll the dough nice and thin.
Cut out the bells,
    cut out the trees,
Cut out the stars—
    this is a breeze!
Into the oven—
    the big hand's on ten.
When it hits twelve,
    take 'em out again.

Busy as a bee, Junior sings
"The First Noel" and "We Three Kings."
Enter Mrs. Kroll! The floor sets her reeling:
Side by side, two broken eggs are staring at the ceiling.
Operation Cleanup. She's silent in her rage,
Until she sees the cookies, looking like a page
From a Fanny Farmer cookbook. Her face turns very red.
"Grandfather's maid, Ruby, taught me how," Junior said.
"When I stayed at Grandfather's house,
    while you and Dad were away,
Ruby baked a batch of cookies
    for the church bazaar each day.
She taught me how, and when I'd learned,
    she let me bake them, too."
Mrs. Kroll said quietly,
"That was a nice thing for Ruby to do."

NEW FRIENDS

Junior Kroll decided to visit
The new next-door neighbors. "Yes, who is it?"
Margaret called as she struggled with the lock.
"It's me, Junior Kroll." He continued to knock.
She opened the door. "Please, come in."
"I'm Junior Kroll." He flashed a grin.
"I live on the other side of those Christmas trees."
"You're our very first guest. Have a seat, please."
Junior was carefully testing each chair
When Max appeared wearing a pair
Of bunny slippers. Junior gasped, "They're just like mine."
"Good," replied Max. "We should get along fine."
"I know something you don't know,"
Max chewed his cigar. "Tell me slow."
"I have a dog with the same name as you."
Max raised his eyebrows. "Is he Jewish, too?'"
Junior snickered. "He's a crazy Great Dane."
Margaret quipped, "This one is also insane."
"Close your mouth, Margaret. You're causing a draft."
Margaret made a face and Junior laughed.
"I almost forgot to tell you that you're invited
For Christmas Eve dinner." The two were delighted.
"I guess I'd better go now. Mom says I'm sometimes a pest."
"I disagree," Max replied. "You're a most interesting guest."
And from that time a path was worn
    through the Christmas trees
That grew between two fine old houses
    and marked the boundaries.

THE ANIMAL SHELTER

Junior Kroll thought Santa Claus
Should visit the animal shelter because
The animals were part of the first Holy Night.
Mom and Dad said that it would be all right
To ask the folks who lived on the street
If they'd like to contribute a toy or a treat.
Junior rang doorbells and the folks came through
With fancy dog biscuits and good things to chew.
There were toys to squeak and balls to roll.
It was four days before Christmas, and Junior Kroll
Arrived at the shelter with the big surprise:
Crazy Max was in disguise,
Wearing white curly whiskers under his chin
And a Santa Claus hat. When Max walked in
Pulling a wagon, everyone cheered,
But poor Crazy Max just kept scratching his beard.
The dogs all barked and the cats meowed,
And Junior Kroll was ever so proud,
Because the folks on his street had decided to share
The joy of Christmas with the animals there.
Then Junior suggested they sing a song,
And the dogs and cats all sang along.

OPERATION FIND THE LOOT

Junior Kroll noticed, at this time of year,
Packages would arrive, then disappear.
Mrs. Kroll explained that Santa's sleigh
Couldn't deliver all the presents by Christmas Day,
So in order to avoid holiday stress,
Sometimes Santa used Federal Express.
Junior, of course, was honor bound
And promised not to go snooping around.
He had every intention of keeping his word,
Until he decided it was really absurd
Not to check and see if Santa had missed
Something on his Christmas list.
It was Junior Kroll in hot pursuit.
Operation . . . Find the Loot!
Wait till opportunity knocks,
Then remove the shoes. Wear only socks.
Here we go, tippy-toe.

Like a cartoon cat, take it nice and slow.
First the attic for a little peek—
Better watch out, those floorboards squeak.
Make it fast, can't stay too long.
Mom's gonna know something's wrong.
There it is—the voice of doom.
"Junior, are you in my room?"
Saved by the phone. She'll be busy a while.
The cartoon cat wears a devilish smile.
Check the closets, leave no clues.
Be careful, don't disturb those shoes.
Nothing here, nothing there,
Under the bed, under the chair.
Meanwhile, Junior doesn't hear Mother say,
"Yes, he's been on the prowl all day."
The cartoon cat is still in hot pursuit,
But Mom knows he'll never find the loot.

TROUBLE IN TOYLAND

Junior Kroll took his cousin, Honey Duff,
In her little fur coat and her little fur muff,
To see Santa Claus at the department store,
While Mom and Aunt Jane shopped another floor.
They entered Toyland and followed the sign
That led them straight to the end of the line,
Where anxious kids waited to chat
With a well-groomed Santa who was naturally fat.
Suddenly, cousin Honey Duff
Hit the boy in front with her little fur muff.
Before Junior could apologize,
The boy pulled Honey's hat over her eyes.
The white woolly hat stretched down to her collar.
Honey staggered about and began to holler.
Ten tall soldiers in a holiday display
Toppled over when they got in her way.
While Junior and the other kid were exchanging blows,
Honey was trying to get the hat past her nose.
She sat on the floor, kicking her feet.
Suddenly, Junior's opponent made a fast retreat,
Leaving Junior to deal with the manager's rage.
No one blamed Honey, because of her age.
On the way home Junior tried to explain
Exactly what happened to Mom and Aunt Jane.
Sitting beside him, cousin Honey Duff,
In her little fur coat and her little fur muff,
There on the backseat with a smile so sweet,
Gave Junior a kick with her tiny little feet.

O LITTLE TOWN OF BETHLEHEM

Junior Kroll got cardboard boxes
    and cut out Three Wise Men.
Working feverishly with crayons and paint,
    he did them over again.
Everything had to be perfect.
    When the stage was finally set,
The library doors swung open
    to music from a failing cassette.
Cousin Honey Duff was cast in the role
Of gentle Mary by director Kroll.
Junior took the part of Joseph,
    and with no crib for a bed,
The Tangerine Bear, wrapped in a blanket,
    lay in a basket instead.

Through the dim light the family saw
A star on the head of Arty, the macaw.
Junior signaled they were about to begin,
When suddenly a crazy camel rushed in.
A pillow for his hump, the Krolls' Great Dane
Grabbed the Tangerine Bear, and Arty went insane.
The star of Bethlehem flew out the door,
And the Three Wise Men lay flat on the floor.
Junior struggled to set them upright,
While gentle Mary engaged in a fight
With the crazy camel over the Tangerine Bear,
Who wound up badly in need of repair.

Then all did their best to try and console
A very disheartened Junior Kroll,
Describing his re-creation of Bethlehem
As a moving event; and they breathed an AMEN.

THE CHOCOLATE PIGS

Junior Kroll saved his nickels and dimes
For presents he wrapped at least fifteen times.
Then he put them all in one big box
Under his bed with his dirty socks.
Junior had counted what he had to spend
And divided the total by ten.
The amount was such that he couldn't buy much,
But he came up with a plan in the end.
He bought ten chocolate pigs, a Christmas treat.
Everybody liked something sweet.

It was Christmas Eve, late afternoon.
The family would be arriving soon.
"Wait till they see my presents," he said.
And kneeling down, he reached under the bed.
But his blood ran cold as the shattered box
Slid out on top of his dirty socks.
The pigs were gone. Not even a trace.
Junior knew Max had fallen from grace.

Junior told the story for the fifteenth time
About the chocolate pigs and Max's crime.
And as he told it, the story got longer;
The pigs got bigger, and the laughter grew stronger.

And the Christmas tree lights burned beautiful and bright,
As they shimmered on the snow outside the window all night.